Puppy Training

Top 10 Ideas For Training Your Dog Within A Month To Keep Everybody In Your House Happy And Stress Free

Other Books by R and R

<u>Meditation for beginners</u>
What is Meditation and how can it change your life? A Guide to mindfulness and happiness.

<u>F*ck Motivation</u>
It's your life. A guide on how to live your life and be happy.

<u>Declutter</u>
A beginners 10 step guide on how to simplify life by decluttering.

<u>New Habits - New Wealth</u>
How changing some habits can improve your personal health and financial wealth.

<u>Puppy Training</u>
Top 10 ideas for training your dog within a month to keep everybody in your house happy and stress free.

<u>Minimalist</u>
The How-To and Why of becoming a minimalist

www.randrdigitallifestyle.com

Introduction

We want to thank you and congratulate you for purchasing the book, *"Puppy Training: Top 10 Ideas For Training Your Dog Within A Month To Keep Everybody In Your House Happy And Stress-Free".*

This book has 10 powerful ideas on how to train your puppy or dog in as little as a month to keep everybody in your house happy and stress-free.

Owning a pet, training it, and seeing it grow into an obedient and valuable member of the family is very fulfilling. Take the example of a dog.

The idea of taking a puppy home, acclimatizing it to its new home, caring for it, potty training it, and teaching it how to obey your commands is likely to fill you and your family—especially if you have kids—with lots of excitement, which is excellent but...

Training your puppy is a very involved process. It requires a detailed plan, loads of patience, and a god-like level of focus and consistency. This guide takes you by the hand and using very detailed prompts, shows you how to train your puppy or dog within a month. By design, the ideas and strategies discussed in this guide are actionable and very easy to implement.

Worth noting: Compared to hiring a professional dog trainer, personally training your puppy is much more effective and fun. In addition to being effective and enjoyable, personally training your puppy establishes you as the alpha, which makes it easier for your puppy or dog to obey you and to integrate well into the home environment.

Let's get started:

Thanks again for purchasing this book. We hope you enjoy it! Ray & Ruby

Table of Content

The Benefits: Is Training Your Puppy Important?

The short and sweet answer is **YES**! Training your puppy to be an obedient and valuable member of your home is important. The sooner you start doing it, the likelier you are to start enjoying the many benefits of being a happy dog owner.

Training your puppy, or rather, acclimatizing your puppy to its new owner and home environment has tons of benefits for you as a dog owner—or as a family that owns a dog—and for the dog itself.

This part of the guide discusses the key benefits of owning a puppy and training it. We shall take a two-pronged approach to these benefits:

1: The Benefits for You

First, having a well-trained puppy/dog keeps everybody in the house—including the puppy/dog—happy and stress-free.

When you train your puppy/dog using the various strategies we shall discuss in this guide, you become a puppy/dog owner who does not deal with common dog owner problems such as teething—for puppies—

chewing on things, excessive barking, chasing, digging, or inappropriate elimination.

In addition, by personally training your puppy/dog, you understand its basic needs better, which makes you capable of providing your puppy/dog with all the forms of care it needs including medical, food, water, and training.

Among many other benefits, training your puppy/dog will:

Help you and your puppy/dog create a deeper bond

Training your puppy/dog will help create a stronger bond between you and your puppy/dog. When you take up puppy/dog training, since you will be spending a substantial amount of time teaching your puppy/dog how to be obedient and how to behave around the home environment, it strengthens the bond between you and your puppy/dog.

Creating a bond with your puppy/dog starts the moment you bring your puppy/dog home. Similarly, training your puppy/dog should start the moment you bring it home. By spending time with your puppy/dog as you train it and acclimatize it to its new home and family, like a human child, as the puppy/dog learns about you, your family, and its new home, it learns to trust and respect you. This mutual bond is very beneficial.

It's a joyful experience

A well-trained puppy/dog is more capable, homely, and a delight to spend time with. The puppy/dog-training experience is also a fun experience for you.

In addition to having fun as you train your puppy/dog, seeing your new puppy/dog become an integral part of your home environment and successfully be in other situations—hotels, the streets, at the park, in the car—will fill you with an immense amount of joy.

A well-trained puppy/dog is the envy of all dog-owners.

Safety

Obedience training is the most foundational of all dog-training strategies. Teaching your puppy/dog how to obey your commands allows you to teach your puppy/dog fun commands such as come, roll over, and fetch, as well as other commands that could very well help you save your dog's life.

Take the example of teaching your puppy/dog how to obey the stop or come commands. These basic commands allow you to control your puppy/dog in whichever situation, including risky ones.

Another fun benefit of training your puppy/dog is that when you do it diligently, and your puppy/dog becomes highly obedient, you can involve your puppy/dog in fun activities—such as a fun day at the park—including ones related to dog sports.

2: The Benefits for Your Puppy

In-home training is highly beneficial to your dog. Among many others, here are some of the benefits of training for your puppy/dog:

Exercise and mental stimulation

For a puppy/dog to remain mentally and physically strong, i.e., for a dog to live a rich life, it needs the basic needs that we all need: food, water, shelter, safety, medical care, and two other things: physical exercises and mental stimulations.

A puppy/dog that does not get enough exercise–even dogs as lazy as the English bulldog need a fair amount of exercise–is likely to engage in anxious behavior such as excessive barking, biting, and begging.

Your dedicated puppy/dog training time is an ideal time to give your puppy/dog the exercise it needs to remain physically and mentally strong. Working with treats to teach your dog commands, you consider important is mentally stimulating for your puppy/dog.

Moreover, when you socialize your puppy/dog— socialization is part of the puppy/dog-training process—the process is both fun as well as physically and mentally stimulating for the puppy/dog.

The dog feels loved and wanted

When your puppy/dog sees how much time you spend with it, teaching it how to behave and live harmoniously within its new home, it feels loved and wanted.

It's important to remember that dogs are pack animals. In the wild, the bitch is responsible for integrating new puppies into the pack environment/home and teaching them how to behave and survive within that environment.

In a modern world setting, for your puppy/dog, you and family members are the pack, and it's, therefore, your responsibility to acclimatize a new puppy/dog to its new home or family. When you dedicate time to doing this, your puppy/dog feels welcome, loved and wanted by its new family, which can have a profound effect on how the puppy/dog behaves in the home and responds to your commands.

Your puppy/dog will be happier

Starting the training process as early as possible allows you to socialize the puppy and teach it good behaviors that can help it successfully navigate the modern world we all live in.

Research has shown that well-trained dogs/puppies are happier because they are less likely to engage in behaviors that are likely to make you unhappy or leave you frustrated.

In addition, spending time with your puppy/dog, which cements your bond, shows the puppy/dog how much you care. A cared-for puppy/dog that's a part of a productive family unit is likely to be happy.

Overall, training your puppy/dog is so beneficial and of such importance that it can be the difference between being a happy or frustrated puppy/dog owner. Always remember that a "bad dog/puppy" is just a puppy/dog that is yet to learn good or appropriate behavior. Training is the difference between a 'good' or 'bad' puppy/dog.

Now that you know the benefits of training your puppy/dog, before we discuss a 10-step simple process that will help you get started, let us lay the groundwork:

#1: Pre-Puppy: Establish Some Ground Rules

Before your puppy joins your home, have in place a defined routine and some ground rules. Create these rules and routines, keeping in mind that once you bring your new puppy or dog home, it will experiment with different behaviors as it acclimatizes to its new home environment.

Establishing some ground rules allows you to control how your puppy learns to behave in your home. It helps you define wanted and unwanted behavior. Once you have these defined, you effectively create a home environment that allows you to teach your dog how to become a well-mannered and trusted member of the household, which translates into less stress for all and a better relationship with your dog.

At a basic level, define the following:

1. Which behaviors—from and towards the dog—are acceptable and which ones are not.

2. A feeding and elimination schedule with a clearly defined structure of who is responsible for the task.

3. Where to create a space that makes your puppy feel safe and welcome—for puppies below one-year-old, creating a space within a well-used area

will help eliminate anxiety and night crying/whining.

4. The words used to command the dog. In general, your family needs to master three main words: ***good***, ***no***, and ***okay***. Use "***Good***"—said joyously and accompanied with fond petting— to communicate wanted behavior. This word communicates your happiness towards a specific behavior exhibited by your dog. You can accompany it with positive reinforcements such as treats, praise, and petting. Use "***No***" to communicate your displeasure for the puppy, making the wrong choice; avoid tying the usage of this word to a punishment. Use "***Okay***" to release your dog from a command. For instance, when teaching the stay command, we would use the word "okay" to communicate that it is now okay for the dog to get out of that position. Learn to use these words consistently and without a doubt, training your puppy will be super easy.

5. Show your kids how to handle the puppy. Make sure you explicitly state that no one should disturb the puppy while it is sleeping—puppies need tons of sleep—or eating, and that there's no teasing the puppy with food or toys, and no yelling at, biting, hitting the puppy, no ear or tail pulling, and no pinching or prodding the puppy.

6. Define whether it is OK for your puppy to be on your sofa, the bed, and other pieces of furniture, accepted and non-accepted games, and where and how the puppy shall be spending most of the waking day. Clearly define who shall be responsible for what—training, feeding, etc.—and reinforce the need for consistent behavior towards the puppy throughout the home environment.

7. Create a growing list of words that all family members can use while communicating with the puppy as it learns new behaviors and becomes a valuable member of the home. You will be the primary trainer, yes, but involving the entire family in the process will make it fun and easier for all to remain consistent with the process and as a family.

8. Define the right way of correcting mistakes and unwanted behavior. Clearly define which methods you and your family shall be using when correcting the puppy's behavior during training sessions and everyday interactions. The first few days, weeks, and months after you bring your puppy home will make all the difference.

9. Establish a sequence of commands. A basic command structure should include three steps: *the command, the obedience*, and finally, *the praise for exhibiting wanted behavior*. Establish how you

will be praising your puppy whenever it exhibits good behavior as well as the vocal commands and body language modes you shall use to display displeasure with a specific habit.

10. Think about what you intend to teach your puppy about going through doors. Teach your puppy how to wait for permission before going through doorways and gates.

These ten ground rules—and any other you may create to match your personal home situation—will help you create a conducive environment that you can use to turn your puppy into a valued and well-mannered member of the family.

Create a feeding, house training, and obedience training schedule

<u>Important Note</u>

Since we have many types of dog breeds, you and your family should aim to learn as much as you can about caring for all dogs but specifically about caring for the type of puppy you want to bring home. In an ideal situation, you should choose to bring home a puppy whose intrinsic characteristics are right for you and your family.

The next step is to gather the supplies you and your puppy shall need for the training sessions, and that is essential to the puppy's stay in your home.

#2: Pre-Puppy: Prepare Your Home and Gather Your Supplies

To house and crate train your puppy, which is the first thing you should teach your puppy the moment you bring it home, you will need supplies such as a crate.

When gathering your supplies for puppy training, aim to create a comfortable space that allows you and your puppy to be happy as you both learn how to adapt to each other within the home environment.

Here is a basic selection of supplies you will need to gather before you bring a new puppy home.

A crate

A crate is an invaluable puppy train tool. On top of being very helpful with house training, it is an ideal way to give your puppy a private space, a sanctuary within the larger home environment. A larger playpen can also act as a crate.

Basic supplies

You need:

1. Food and water dishes

2. A crate, which we noted is essential.

3. An ideal type of food as well as tasty treats used during the behavior training process

4. Beddings, a brush, and comb

5. Chew toys and other kinds of toys

6. A quality nail trimmer and the other grooming supplies you need to keep your puppy's fur healthy

7. Collar and ID tags

8. A Clicker

9. Grooming tools

10. Important house cleaning tools

Prepare a home for your puppy and Puppy-proof your home

To create a home for your puppy within the broader home area, choose an area of your home, and use it to create a gated-off home for your puppy.

In a family household, an ideal location for a puppy's home is the kitchen or any other area that gets a lot of activity from everyone within the household. This helps the puppy feel part of a larger family instead of isolated and lonely. Creating a gated-off area for your dog also ensures that as you endeavor to train your puppy, you also have a safe area where you can place the puppy whenever you are not training it or supervising it within the broader home environment.

Puppies react differently to new environments; some will take to mischievous exploring, others will be meek and cower in a corner for some time. Whatever the case may be with your puppy, before you bring it home, you need to be deliberate about creating a safe home environment. This is where puppy proofing your home comes in.

Move detergents and other cleaning supplies to someplace out of reach. Keep your trash wraps/cans covered and secure, wrap all your electrical cords in sturdy cord covers, move house plants if need be, and do whatever else you need to do to ensure the puppy's new home environment is safe.

Find a vet

Once home, your puppy will need proper medical care, vaccines, annual checkup, etc. Find a vet that lives close by and a pet medical center that operates 24 hours. Pin this emergency number on the refrigerator and ensure that everyone in the house knows what to do in case of an emergency.

With the pre-puppy phase done, you can now move to the post-puppy training phase that starts with bringing your puppy home:

#3: The Right Way to Bring a New Puppy Home

From the onset, your communication with the puppy should be clear and consistent. Like a human child, puppies learn best when the consequences of a behavior are immediate. If your puppy does something that leads to any form of reward—food, a snack, a treat, or even a petting—it is likely to repeat that behavior. If the puppy does something that immediately leads to an unpleasant consequence, it is then unlikely to repeat that behavior or start performing the behavior less.

Picking up your puppy

For the car ride home, a comfortable crate is ideal because it provides a safe space for the puppy. If you are picking your puppy from a breeder, have the breeder introduce the puppy to the crate a few days before you bring your puppy home with you or to give you some form of material—may be a blanket or newspapers—that has the scent of the puppy's previous home. This is especially helpful as a stop-gap measure for loneliness once your puppy gets home and you introduce it to its crate<see crate training.

If you are taking home a very young puppy, remember to pick up and handle the puppy with gentle care. Remind everyone in the home not to pick up the puppy unless it's absolutely necessary. Go a step further and create a step-like list of how to pick up the puppy—you can stick this list on the refrigerator, perhaps next to the feeding and training schedule.

- Step 1: Place one hand under your puppy's rump and place your other hand under his chest.

- Step 2: Lift with both arms. With a small adult dog, use the puppy technique. For larger dogs, wrap both arms around his legs; draw him to your chest, and lift.

Keep the car ride home relaxed and as quiet as possible, and because puppies tend to get car sick, line the crate or your car upholstery with a paper sheet or towels.

The puppy is also likely to whine on the car ride home. If it does, do not reward the behavior by petting the puppy nor punish it by admonishing the behavior. If you keep the environment calm, the situation will self-diffuse.

If during the ride home, your puppy gets too whiny, unruly, or noisy, place the puppy between your feet;

the den-like area will calm the puppy so that you can get it home.

Once you get home

Immediately after the ride from the breeder or pet store, take the puppy out to a pre-designated potty area such as a backyard or an area set up on the balcony of an apartment, and when the puppy relieves itself, offer some praise, and perhaps a treat—any form of pre-chosen reward will do.

When introducing the puppy to the indoors of your home and to your family, make sure the environment is calm and pleasant; encourage the avoidance of over-excitement.

Keep in mind that the puppy will need a fair amount of time to adjust to you and its new home environment. Once inside the house, leash the puppy, and show it around the home; hold onto the leash lightly as the puppy moves from one area to the other.

If you would rather not leash the puppy on its first day home, you can choose to sit on the floor with it as you pet it as you talk to it to get it accustomed to your voice.

Because puppies have underdeveloped bladders, take the puppy out after every 15-20 minutes of excitement or play and shortly after every meal. Get into the habit of taking your puppy out to potty the last thing in the evening and first thing in the morning.

After going to potty, play with your puppy (or train it) for 5-10 minutes making sure to use positive reinforcement for wanted behavior. Remember that puppies, and all dogs for that matter, learn best when the consequences of their behavior are immediate.

After introducing your puppy to its new home, if you did not carry it home in its crate, introduce the puppy to its crate by offering it its food or treats within the crate. Do not force your puppy into the crate; that will do you no good. Just place food or treats in the crate, sit close by, and watch as your puppy finds its way around and into its crate for exploration. Remember to keep the crate in an area that gets a lot of activity; this will keep the puppy from feeling lonely.

For the first few days and weeks, keep the mood calm and supervise all explorative journeys into the larger home environment but make sure your puppy knows where to find its water and food bowl, which areas are off limit and the puppy bathroom—we shall cover that in crate and house training.

Create a predictable routine for your puppy (and yourself). Feed your puppy at the same time each day, house train it at the same time—this is only necessary for the first few weeks of bringing your puppy home—and play with it or take the puppy out for a walk at the same time each day. Creating a routine beforehand is an invaluable puppy-training tool.

Create a schedule that clearly defines potty breaks, training times, meal times, nap times, play times, and sleeping and wake up times. A predictable routine makes it relatively easy to train your puppy as quickly as possible.

Start training your puppy the moment you bring it home. Crate and house training are the first things you should start doing immediately after bringing your puppy home.

#4: Post-Puppy: Crate Train Your Puppy

As mentioned, a crate is an invaluable training and behavior management tool in puppies. The earlier you start using it, the easier it shall be to house train your puppy and teach it good manners—as well as basic commands.

If you did not bring your puppy home in its crate, after taking the puppy out for a potty session, which you should do before taking it into the house, immediately introduce your puppy to its crate.

Before introducing your puppy to the crate, make sure it's homey and comfortable. You can do this using old blankets and towels. To keep the puppy from feeling lonely, place the blanket with the "smell of home" in the crate. Make sure you give your puppy its food in the crate.

The crate training process does not take a single day; the length of the process is individual and depends on factors such as your approach, your dog's temperament, and experiences.

The secret to acing crate training is to ensure your approach to the process is one that allows you to help the puppy associate the crate with security and a sense of home.

As mentioned earlier, place the crate in an area of your home that gets a lot of activity, such as the kitchen or family room.

To introduce the puppy to the crate in a way that ensures it feels comfortable and secure, dedicate a bit of time to introducing the puppy to the crate. An ideal way to do this is by, immediately after letting the dog indoors, placing some treats in the crate and allowing the puppy to explore the crate willingly.

If your puppy does not willingly explore the crate when you place treats in there, offer the puppy its food at the mouth of the crate and keep moving the food and water bowls further until they are finally inside the crate and the puppy can get in and out of the crate at will.

If you intend to turn the crate into a safe environment that the puppy can stay in when you are not supervising it during home and obedience training sessions, once the puppy has positive sentiments towards the crate, start closing the doorway for shorter periods at first.

When the puppy can comfortably feed within the crate, close the door and stand nearby so that you can open it immediately after the puppy finishes its meal. After that, play with the puppy (or train it) for 10-15 minutes and then take it out to potty in the designated area. When the puppy defecates, reward it.

Keep crating the puppy for a longer period at a time, and each time you place the puppy in the crate, use an accompanying command such as "crate" or "kennel." When the puppy can comfortably use the crate without signs of anxiety, use the "crate" or "kennel" command to crate the puppy for a shorter period when you are at home.

How to Teach your Puppy the Crate Command

To introduce your puppy to the crate and teach it the "crate" command at the same time, stand by the crate, treat in hand (or some treats within the crate), and use the command word crate while pointing to the crate. When the puppy enters the crate, offer some praise and treats—if you are using a clicker, you can use it to cue good behavior.

Repeat this process as many times as it takes to teach your puppy to go to its crate by command and to stay there for longer periods. As the puppy gets used to staying in the crate for longer—this will depend on your routine—wean the puppy of the need for treats to obey the crate command.

Crate training has two main problem areas: separation, anxiety, and whining. If crating your puppy leads to incessant whining and separation anxiety even when you do not reward the behavior, try to ignore the puppy but only if you are sure the puppy is not hungry or in need of eliminating. If the problem persists, start the crate training process from the start or consult a professional.

After your puppy becomes comfortable with staying in the crate for longer, say overnight without any problem, the next step is house training the puppy or introducing it to the larger home environment.

#5: Post Puppy: House Train Your Puppy

House training your puppy is an involved process that requires consistent positive reinforcement from the onset. The idea behind house training your puppy is to ensure that your puppy has proper toilet etiquette and mannerism within the broader home area.

Fully house training a puppy takes 4-6 months with the success of the process pinned on your ability to stay consistent with your routine and schedule. At the heart of the process is ensuring that your puppy can comfortably fit into your broader home environment without the fear of unsupervised defection.

For smaller puppy breeds, keep in mind that these puppies have small bladders and because they are active more, they need more bathroom breaks in between meals, treats, and training sessions.

Because the process takes longer and is, therefore, more involved, be patient with yourself, especially since you are likely to make many mistakes. The trick is to keep going past the mistakes and remaining constant with a determined course of action.

When to Start House Training

Start house training your puppy immediately after bringing the puppy home. The expert recommendation is to start potty training a puppy once it turns 12 weeks old—make sure the puppy you take home is 12-16 weeks old—at which point the puppy has a small but established sense of bladder control.

House training a puppy that is older than 12 weeks old will take longer, and require a more delicate and detailed approach, especially if the puppy in question has been defecating in a crate.

How to House Train Your Puppy

According to professional dog experts and trainers, the best way to start house training your puppy is to start by creating a space you can use to confine the puppy; a crate is an ideal example.

As you feed your puppy regularly, train/play with it, and then take it out to its potty area, your puppy will learn to hold it in or signal you when it needs relief. By controlling when your puppy does its business and denying it meals in between your feeding schedule, you minimize the risk of potty training accident and mishaps.

Start the house training process on the first day by showing your puppy its potty area. Take your puppy out to a designated potty area first thing in the morning and continue taking the puppy to the designated area every 30-45 minutes but especially after feedings, play times, and training sessions.

Take your puppy to the potty area before you all turn in for the night and after every nap. Take your puppy to the same potty area, and every time it eliminates, offer praise, and a treat. You can also tie the command word, "potty" to being in this area.

Although there are many ways to house train a puppy, crate training is the best especially immediately after you bring your puppy home; as the puppy grows older, you can choose a potty spot located outside.

Using a crate to house train, your puppy makes it easier to recognize when the puppy shows signs of needing bladder relief. To use a crate for house training, make sure it's big enough for the puppy to lie down, stand, and comfortably turn around in but not too big that the puppy gets into the habit of using one corner of the crate for potty purposes.

Signs of a puppy in need of eliminating

In addition to taking your puppy out the last thing at night, first thing in the morning, after every 30-45 minutes, 15-minutes after feeding and play/training sessions, and after every nap, take your puppy out when it shows signs such as whining, sniffing and clawing the ground, circling and barking.

House training your puppy is likely to be a process full of setbacks until your puppy is a year old and well trained and house broken. Be mindful of potty accidents and your reaction to them. Most potty training accidents are a result of failure to adhere to a schedule, a change of environment, or incomplete house training.

To avoid these problems, do not punish your puppy for accidents you notice long after the puppy has done its business. Remember that puppies learn best when the consequences of their behavior are immediate. When you come home to find that your puppy has defecated outside the potty area, clean it with a strong enzymatic cleanser that masks the scent; do not punish your puppy for that behavior.

If you catch your puppy in the act of eliminating, call out to the puppy loudly but not too loudly that you scare it or clap, leash the puppy, take it out to the designated potty area, encourage it to "go potty," and reward the puppy with praise and a treat immediately after it eliminates within the designated potty area.

As you teach your puppy how to navigate around the larger home situation without causing potty accidents, you should also embark on leash training, which is the next idea you should implement:

#6: Post-Puppy: Leash Train the Puppy

Accustoming your puppy to a leash is a great way to ensure that as your puppy grows and matures, it grows into a dog that can successfully follow the command to walk nicely on a leash.

Since a dog's primary instinct is to be free, when you attach a leash to a dog and then pull, the puppy is likely to pull back, which can make leash training more difficult than it need be.

To get started with leash training process quickly and effortlessly, do the following:

1. Be mindful of how you introduce the puppy and the leash. Your aim should be to ensure that the puppy does not attach negative connotations to the leash. Before you attach a leash, start by ensuring your puppy is comfortable with wearing a collar. You can attach the collar when you are playing with the puppy and giving it treats for good behavior. When the puppy is comfortable with the collar, attach the leash, and let the puppy drag it around for a bit before taking the other end and following it around.

2. The next step is to teach the puppy a cue that allows it to know that you are about to give it food

or a treat. You can use the puppy's name or other cue words such as "here boy or girl." The idea is to use the cue word/s while in a quiet setting and when the puppy looks at you or turns towards you, to reward the puppy with a treat or food; after doing this several times, the puppy should start coming towards you every time you use the cue word.

3. As the puppy is coming to you with the leash still attached and dragged around, move back a few paces, call again, and when the puppy comes to you, offer positive reinforcement—a treat or petting. Repeat this several times—and keep the training sessions short—until your puppy can come to you every time you use the cue word and walk to you when you move a few paces back.

4. After your pup understands the concept of coming to you when you call—this is a great way to teach your puppy to respond to a given name—move to a distraction-free indoor area, take the unattached edge of the leash, and start walking; do not pull the puppy. When you notice some resistance, stop, call the puppy to your side, move a few paces back, and when the puppy comes to you, offer some treats and praise.

5. As the puppy gets used to walking with you on a slacked leash, offer treats and vocal/non-vocal

praise whenever the puppy walks close to your side and tie this behavior to a cue such as "walk nicely" or "by my side."

6. When the puppy can comfortably walk by your side for a few minutes while indoors, repeat the cue, behavior, and reward process until your puppy can walk by your side on command—remember to keep training sessions short and fun for the puppy.

7. When you feel ready and are sure your puppy now accepts you as its natural leader, you can take your puppy out for an experimental leashed walk in the great outdoors. Because of the distractions present in the outdoors, carry lots of treats, and whenever your puppy falls behind, rather than tug or pull on the leash, stop, call your him/her to you, move a few paces back, and when it comes to you, offer a reward or any form of positive reinforcement. Repeat this process as many times as it takes your puppy to learn to walk nicely on a leash by command.

Common Leash Training Problems

When leash training a puppy, be on the lookout for the following problems and seek to proof against them so that your puppy/dog consistently learns how to walk nicely on a leash as it grows into an adult, well-behaved dog.

1. Pulling: It's very likely that even after your puppy learns to walk nicely on a leash, there will be instances when it pulls ahead or in a direction opposite the intended one. As mentioned earlier, when this happens, do not engage the puppy in a tug of war. Instead, stand rooted without moving, use the cue word to call the puppy to your side, and when he/she comes back to you, offer a treat or any other form of positive reinforcement. If your puppy is a chronic puller, consider using a head halter or a front-hook harness.

2. Lunging: When you start taking your pup out for walks outside, chances are that it will lunge after things such as a running kid, a car, and other dogs. When this happens, again, remain deeply rooted like a strong oak tree and try to recapture the pup's attention with a cue word and a treat.

3. Incessant barking: Depending on the breed, your pup is also likely to bark at people and other dogs whenever you take it out for a walk. A lack of socialization and enough exercise are often the leading cause of this behavior. Give your puppy enough exercise and mental stimulation depending on breed.

As your puppy learns how to walk nicely on a leach, you can teach it other skills such as heel where you teach him/her to walk in the heel position, at knee level on your left side, with the ability to start and stop walking when you do.

Leash training is a lifelong process. After your puppy learns to come to you and walk nicely on a leash, consistently take it out for walks and remain consistent with the process so that you can reinforce the behavior and easily overcome challenges.

Consider using a clicker as part of your puppy-training program:

#7: Post-Puppy: Clicker Training

First, a clicker is a small handheld device that upon use, makes a very distinct sound that attracts a puppy's/dog's attention. Clicker training is an effective positive reinforcement strategy you can use alongside commands, treats, and any other form of positive reinforcement.

The ideology behind clicker training is simple: when you give your puppy a command that the puppy obeys, you press the clicker and offer a treat and lots of praise. As you consistently use the clicker in this command, click, and reward system, your puppy learns to associate the click with good behavior and the reward that follows.

The secret to clicker training success

To achieve effortless success with clicker training, get the clicker timing right. Keep in mind that in most cases, a reward follows a click, and as such, the clicker aims to ensure that your dog successfully relates the behavior to the click and reward. Click immediately after your puppy displays the desired behavior. For instance, if you are conducting an obedience training sessions where your puppy sits on command, click, treat and praise immediately after your pup sits so that the puppy relates the good behavior the click and the reward.

Simple Steps to Clicker Training Success

To ensure your clicker training process starts on the right foot, implement the following steps/strategies:

1. Introduce the clicker: The best way to introduce a clicker to your puppy is to be on the lookout for instances when your puppy voluntarily engages in good behavior and when these behaviors manifest, clicking and rewarding the puppy. For example, when you notice your puppy voluntarily making the motion to sit, click the moment the pup's butt touches the floor and then offer a reward. Couple the clicking and positive reinforcement with an appropriate cue word such as sit.

2. Load the clicker: "Loading" or explaining the meaning of the click hastens the clicker training process. To load the clicker, place small bits of tasty, smelly treats in a shallow dish meant for your puppy. Sit comfortably on the floor with the dish within easy reach but out of the pup's reach. Pick up one piece of treat in one hand with the clicker in the other hand. Immediately after the

puppy pays attention or comes to investigate the nice smell, click and offer the treat and some encouragement/petting.

3. Repeat: Repeat the behavior>click>and treat sequence at least 10-12 times in a row. Your puppy should quickly learn to associate the click with a treat. With the clicker loaded, you can then use the clicker to teach your puppy other behaviors and commands.

As mentioned, clicker-training success depends on your timing. Click and reward as your puppy is engaging in wanted behavior. Young puppies have an innate ability to understand cause and effect. By acing the clicker timing, your puppy will soon start engaging in all sorts of good behaviors in an attempt to hear the click and get the reward that comes after.

As your ability to use the clicker improves, start using the clicker and other forms of positive reinforcement to teach your puppy how to obey your commands, which we call obedience training.

#8: Post-Puppy: Obedience Training

The essence of obedience training is to teach your puppy to respond to cues or commands. The process teaches your puppy how to behave within the broader home environment.

Teaching your puppy how to respond to basic commands is the heart of the process. Start teaching your puppy how to be obedient, or rather, how to obey basic commands such as sit or stay, immediately after you bring it home.

To teach your puppy basic commands, you only need eagerness, patience, some treats, and a clicker—if you are using one. The process of teaching your puppy necessary obedience skills remains unchanged irrespective of the behavior you want to adopt whether it is, sit, leave it, stay, down, or any other basic command.

Template: How to Teach Your Puppy Basic Commands

The template offered here is for teaching your puppy the sit command, but you can customize it to any behaviors or skills you would like to teach your puppy:

1. Load the clicker by catching your puppy in the act of sitting down voluntarily, click the moment the pup's butt touches the floor, and offer a treat or reward. Repeat this 5-10 times.

2. If you would rather not wait until your puppy sits voluntarily, take the puppy out to a quiet area, enclose a treat in your hand, move the treat closer to the pup's mouth, let the puppy sniff the treat and notice it, and immediately start moving your hand away from the pup's snout in an upwards motion. This will prompt the puppy to sit to elongate its neck. The moment the pup's butt touches the floor, click and offer a reward and some praise. Repeat the process several times until your puppy associates the behavior to the click and treat, and make sure you tie the behavior to a cue word such as sit—or the name of the behavior you want to reinforce.

3. Once your puppy accustoms to the clicker and verbal cue for the specific command you are teaching—sit in this case—gradually ease off using a treat but continue using the cue. For instance, you can ask your puppy to sit before you offer it food.

You can use this process to teach your puppy other basic commands such as come, leave it, stop, or rollover.

When using positive reinforcement to teach your puppy how to obey commands, remember to remain consistent, patient, and not to punish your dog for inconsistent behavior; display your displeasure yes, which you can do by withholding treats and taking away toys, but do not punish the puppy. Eventually, your puppy will learn more about the behaviors that make you happy (and the ones that make you unhappy), and will naturally want to avoid behaviors that make you unhappy and that lead to negative consequences such as withheld affection.

#9: Post Puppy: Socialize Your Puppy with Humans and Other Dogs

A family puppy needs to be able to navigate the broader home environment; this is the essence of socialization. Socializing your puppy means equipping the pup with the ability to interact peacefully with human beings and other pets you may have at home.

In addition to exposing your puppy to diverse environments, socializing a puppy also allows you to mold a puppy into a dog that accepts petting from strangers and to meet other dogs without the encounter turning ugly.

Start socializing your puppy immediately after you bring it home. Depending on how old your puppy is at the time of bringing it home, you can also bring home a socialized pup—pups learn how to socialize when they are 7 weeks-4 months old.

How to Socialize a Puppy

Socializing your puppy should start the moment you bring it home. As mentioned earlier, the puppy's first day home should be low-key and devoid of overexcitement.

In the initial days of your puppy's stay at home, introduce the pup to family members, new places, new sounds, smells, and sights; you can do this by supervising the puppy—especially if the puppy is not completely house trained—as it explores the new environment. Be patient with the puppy as you introduce it to new environments and people and remember to take the puppy out for potty after each bout of excitement.

Remember to keep all new experiences positive and to pace yourself lest you move too fast and make mistakes. Whenever you introduce the puppy to a new environment, person, or pet, be keen enough to notice good behavior and remember to click and reward the puppy immediately after it displays the correct behavior. Creating a positive environment is especially important when you are introducing a puppy to a resident dog.

Involve the family in the socialization process. Have different members of the family teaching the puppy the same thing, feeding it, taking it out for walks, and introducing it to new environments and people.

More importantly, go slow, especially when introducing your puppy to new house pets or taking it into public spaces. For example, to get your puppy accustomed to petting from different members of the family, start with a few people, and then continuously introduce other members- one or two at a time.

To socialize your puppy with other dogs, once trained and obedient enough to follow basic commands, especially those that help with management such as sit, come, stop, etc., consider taking the puppy out to the park or enrolling the puppy for socialization classes within your area.

When socializing your puppy, remember that consistency and caution are the secret ingredients to success. The more you encourage your pup to explore and welcome new experiences, which you do by rewarding good behavior within new environments, the more open your puppy shall be too unfamiliar places, objects, and people.

Every time you teach your puppy something new, you have to engage in behavior proofing.

#10: Post-Puppy: Behavior Proofing

Behavior proofing is about repeating the lessons you are teaching your puppy until they become second nature, and the puppy can perform these behaviors on command in challenging situations. Behavior proofing is usually the last step in the dog training process.

Behavior proofing is important because dogs cannot generalize. In one situation, your dog may sit on command while in another situation, saying the command may not lead to the desired behavior. Behavior proofing is about teaching your dog how to respond to cues, in the same way, irrespective of circumstance.

How to Proof Behaviors in a Puppy

The most effective way to proof specific behaviors in your puppy is by practicing commands and the specific behaviors you want to proof in different settings and circumstances. This requires you to cue, click, and treat good behaviors in a new environment.

Think of it this way.

When you are teaching a new command, the advice of this book is to do so in a calm environment. Once your puppy learns the proper way to respond to a cue while in this environment, you can then start 'proofing' or teaching the puppy the same behavior in different circumstances and in the presence of distractions.

Here is a sit template to help you with this:

1. Practice the sit command until your puppy learns to respond to the sit command.

2. Once it starts comprehending this command, start adding other elements such as distractions—perhaps a family member walking into the room—into the environment. As your dog masters the command in new environments, continually add distractions and keep practicing using the cue, click, and reward sequence until the behavior takes root completely. Remember to keep training sessions short (10-5 minutes).

The idea behind proofing is to train your dog how to respond to your commands while in diverse situations. You will know you have successfully proofed a behavior when your dog can perform the desired behavior while in any situation.

Bonus: A 30-Day Puppy Training Time Table

To create an effective 30-day puppy-training schedule, create a 1-day schedule that integrates the ten ideas we have discussed here and then replicate this over 30 days making changes and improvements when necessary and as your dog learns.

Replicate this Daily Schedule over 30 days

Here is a daily sample schedule you can do for 30 days and customize according to your training and family needs:

1. Before bringing your puppy home, create a wake-up and sleeping schedule. For instance, you can wake up the puppy at 6 am and tune out for the night at 10pm.

2. House/potty training: Immediately after waking up, take the puppy to a designated toilet area, and immediately after the puppy eliminates, click and reward—deliver the treat within 3 seconds. From waking up to the point of taking the puppy out for potty should be about 10 or so minutes.

3. From 6:10am-7:00am, feed the puppy within its crate—this is crate training. If your puppy is comfortable being in the crate for longer, you can offer it its food, and as it munches, you can close the crate's door and take a shower. Make sure you command the puppy to sit before you offer it the food—every interaction with your puppy is a fun training opportunity.

4. After the puppy eats, train it, or play with it for 10-15 minutes and then take it out for potty; offer a treat and some praise when the pup 'goes.' Because the puppy will not be hungry after eating, use special treats to keep the puppy interested in the training.

5. If you are leash training, attach the leash and stay close by or tie it to yourself as the puppy explores its new environment. You can also use this time as playtime by offering the puppy a toy, throwing it around and asking the puppy to fetch—make sure to reward the pup whenever it displays wanted behavior.

6. After the play session, take your puppy out to potty and shortly after, out for a walk.

7. In the weeks after bringing your puppy home, accustom it to staying in the crate for longer periods so that after taking the pup out for a walk and a potty session, you can place it in the crate for

a nap as you work or complete other responsibilities. Ensure the puppy has water and a chew toy.

8. At lunch, give the puppy some food and then take it outside to potty and for a longer walk. You can use this time outside to teach and proof new behaviors. Remember to click and give the puppy a treat every time it engages in positive behavior. You can place the puppy in a crate for the afternoon; remember to offer a chew toy.

9. Immediately after the puppy wakes up from a nap, take it out to potty and offer a reward when it does.

10. In the evening, give the puppy food in its crate and after that, play with the puppy for a bit, train it for 10-15 minutes, and then take it out to potty.

11. From 7PM to say 10PM, supervise the puppy as it adventures out into the house—supervising it and noticing signs of elimination will help you avoid potty mistakes.

12. Before heading off to sleep, take the pup out for a short walk and go potty, and immediately after, place the puppy in its crate for the night without fusing over the prospect or being overexcited. In the first few days of the puppy being home, keeps

its night crate within your bedroom or the kid's bedroom so that the puppy does not feel lonely.

Repeat this daily schedule over 30 days, making sure to customize it as necessary, and without a doubt, within those 30-days, you will have successfully created the roadmap you need to have in place to turn your puppy into an obedient, mature dog.

Conclusion

We have come to the end of the book. Thank you for reading and congratulations on reading until the end.

As you have seen, training your puppy may be complicated, it may require a lot of patience and consistency, but it's far from difficult. Using the 10 ideas we have discussed in this guide, you can easily turn any puppy into a well-mannered, valuable member of your home.

If you found the book valuable, can you recommend it to others? One way to do that is to post a review on Amazon.

Thank you, and good luck! Ray & Ruby